MAY - 2015

Ancient Civilizations

Published by Creative Paperbacks
P.O. Box 227, Mankato, Minnesota 56002
Creative Paperbacks is an imprint of
THE CREATIVE COMPANY
www.thecreativecompany.us

Design and production by CHRISTINE VANDERBEEK
Art direction by RITA MARSHALL

Printed in the United States of America

PHOTOGRAPHS BY Corbis (Stefano Bianchetti, Corbis,
Hoberman Collection, National Geographic Society,
Michael Nicholson, Gianni Dagli Orti, Paul Panayiotou,
Stapleton Collection/ADAGP, Vanni Archive),
Newscom (akg-images, World History Archive),
Shutterstock (Anastasios71, Bienchen-s, gallimaufry),
SuperStock (Aristidis Vafeiadakis/age fotostock, The
Art Archive, ClassicStock.com, Robert Harding Picture
Library, Travel Pix Collection/Jon Arnold Images)

LIBRARY OF CONGRESS
CATALOGING-IN-PUBLICATION DATA
Bodden, Valerie.
Greece / by Valerie Bodden.
p. cm. — (Ancient civilizations)
Includes bibliographical references and index.
SUMMARY: A historical overview of the Greek civilization
from the perspectives of the social classes, from the aris-
tocrats to the slaves, including the Mediterranean city-
states' growth and decline.

ISBN 978-1-60818-393-7 (HARDCOVER)
ISBN 978-0-89812-980-9 (PBK)
1. Greece—Civilization—To 146 B.C.—Juvenile literature. I. Title.

DF77.B638 2014
938—dc23   2013032513

CCSS: RI.5.1, 2, 3, 5, 6, 8, 9; RH.6-8.4, 5, 6, 7, 8, 9

FIRST EDITION
9 8 7 6 5 4 3 2 1

GREECE

VALERIE BODDEN

Greece

TABLE OF CONTENTS

INTRODUCTION

The roots of the ancient Greek civilization go back more than 3,500 years, when ancestors of the Greeks, known as the Mycenaeans, first settled in Greece. The Mycenaean culture flourished until about 1200 B.C. when it was wiped out—from internal conflict, invasion, or a disaster such as drought. Greece then entered a period known as the Dark Age. Greek-speaking peoples from the north moved south across the Greek mainland. The surviving Mycenaeans joined these newcomers in many areas, forming a new Greek culture.

Soon, the Greeks began to expand their reach. They settled on neighboring islands such as Crete, the Cycladic Islands, and Sicily. The Greek civilization

The entrance to the Mycenaeans' fortress, called the Lion Gate, still stands today.

eventually reached Italy, southern France, the western coast of Asia Minor (present-day Turkey), and Africa. Everywhere the Greeks went, they spread their culture—including their language, arts, religion, and ideas.

ANCIENT GREECE

Although today we speak of ancient Greece as a single culture, by about 750 B.C., Greece was divided into a number of separate political regions known as city-states. Each city-state consisted of a city, along with the villages and farmland that surrounded it. Scholars estimate that ancient Greece may have been made up of as many as 1,500 separate city-states. Among the largest and most powerful city-states were Athens and Sparta. These two have supplied most of the information modern scholars have about the ancient Greek culture.

Each city-state had its own government, and city-states spent much of their time warring with one another. Even so, trade, religion, and athletic competitions led to the development of a common Greek culture, shared by the people of nearly every city-state.

Most city-states also observed similar social divisions. At the top were a small number of wealthy, landowning *aristocrats*. Aristocrats made up the best-armed warriors in the military and often served as priests in the temples of various gods. Commoners, on the other hand, worked small farms, made crafts, or participated in trade. At the bottom of the social scale were foreigners and slaves.

Despite such social distinctions, Greeks of all classes came together for special events, such as religious festivals or athletic contests. Although people of various classes might interact to some degree, it was rare for a Greek of a lower social class to improve his standing in society. In general, a Greek born to one social class remained in that class his entire life.

Spartan legend told of a boy who hid a stolen fox under his tunic rather than confess.

EVEN AS SMALL

CHILDREN, SPARTAN

BOYS WERE TRAINED

NOT TO CRY, NOT TO

FEAR THE DARK, AND

NOT TO BE PICKY EATERS.

HOLDING THE POWER

Over the course of nearly 1,500 years, most city-states' form of government changed many times. At some point in their history, most city-states went through periods of monarchy, **oligarchy**, **tyranny**, and democracy. As governments changed, so too, did the power of various groups of people.

From the earliest times, the Mycenaean people throughout most of Greece were divided into political units centered on a palace. Each palace was ruled by a king who also controlled the surrounding region. Tombs from this period indicate the elite status of kings and other aristocrats; the bodies of the wealthiest were covered with gold for burial.

Mycenaeans buried their noble dead with funerary masks similar to those of ancient Egypt.

After the collapse of the Mycenaean civilization, most Greek monarchies were replaced by oligarchies. An oligarchy is controlled by a small group of people. In ancient Greece, that group consisted of aristocrats. Most aristocrats were large landowners who inherited their aristocratic, or noble, status from their parents.

Aristocrats were able to maintain control because they defended their subjects from outside invaders. But with the development of city-states in the 800s and 700s B.C., many commoners gained new wealth through trade and manufacturing. Some of them earned enough money to purchase weapons and armor and serve as warriors. These warriors were known as hoplites, and they soon became not only a military group but also a political class. Because hoplites were not from aristocratic families, they had no power in the government, and tensions mounted between the social groups. Beginning in the 650s B.C., hoplites in many city-states supported the overthrow of the ruling aristocrats in favor of tyrants, or rulers who seized power illegally.

Most tyrants were aristocrats, but they

appealed to the masses by bringing an end to fighting among aristocratic families, constructing impressive public buildings, holding lavish festivals, and expanding trade. By the 500s and 400s B.C., however, many tyrants had become oppressive rulers who used force against their people.

When the tyrants were finally overthrown, many of the city-states turned to a new form of government that gave the power to ordinary people: democracy. Athens, for example, became a democracy around 508 B.C. Now power was in the hands of people classified as citizens. In general, a person had to be born in Athens to an Athenian father (later, both parents had to be Athenian) to become a citizen. As a result, only about 6 to 10 percent of Athens's population was likely made up of citizens.

Adult male citizens from all social classes were members of the assembly, a governing body which elected leaders and voted on issues such as whether to sign *treaties* or declare war. The assembly met about 40 times every year, and Athenian citizens considered it their duty to attend meetings. For those who lived in the countryside,

Plato invoked the image of a ship in need of command to explain his views on government.

Did You Know?

A 500-FOOT-HIGH
(152.4 M) HILL IN THE
CENTER OF ATHENS
KNOWN AS THE
ACROPOLIS HELD
MANY IMPORTANT
TEMPLES, INCLUDING
THE PARTHENON.

however, it wasn't always possible to get to Athens. As a result, only about 6,000 men (out of a possible 30,000 to 40,000) might make it to each meeting of the assembly. Anyone in attendance was allowed to speak about any issue that was brought before the assembly. After the discussion, if a vote was required, it was taken by a show of hands. Everyone's vote counted equally.

A separate group, known as the Council of 500, chose which topics would come before the assembly. Members of the Council were selected through a lottery of male citizens aged 18 or older. Around 462 B.C., members of the Council began to receive payment, which meant that even poorer members of society could take time out from their work to serve. At first, Athenian magistrates, or government officials, were elected. Later, however, even these positions were chosen by lottery. Each magistrate performed a specific duty, such as overseeing the treasury or controlling the marketplace.

Democracy lasted nearly 200 years in Athens. But in the mid-300s B.C., Macedonia, a kingdom to the north of Greece, conquered the Greek city-states. This marked the beginning of the Hellenistic period, named for the word the Greeks used to describe themselves: Hellenes. During this time, the Macedonians carried the Greek culture to Egypt, Persia, and other lands they had conquered. Greek aristocrats moved to these Hellenistic kingdoms and served in the newly established governments there. Though the Greek city-states were subject to rule by the Hellenistic powers, the city-states also kept some measure of independence. Most reverted to oligarchies. With the rise of the aristocracy once again, the divide between rich and poor became ever wider.

While most other city-states were experiencing changes in government, Sparta's government remained stable for most of its history. That form of government combined elements of monarchy, oligarchy, and democracy. At the head of the government were two kings who ruled together and had control over the army. A group of officials chosen from among the aristocracy proposed legislation. In addition, all male citizens aged 30 and older voted in the assembly, which had limited powers. All citizens were technically considered equal, but eventually a gap began to open between the rich and the poor of this city-state as well.

The Athenian politician Pericles oversaw construction at the Acropolis (opposite).

LIFE OF LEISURE

In most of Greece, aristocrats were defined by their large, inherited landholdings. That did not mean, however, that the aristocrats lived on and worked their farmland. Instead, they lived in a town or village and had slaves or **tenant** farmers to work their land. The aristocrats collected the income earned from the land.

Because they did not have to work, aristocrats had plenty of time for leisure. Many spent a good deal of their time in the agora, a city-state's central market and gathering place. There they might participate in political debates and **philosophical** discussions. Because they had so much free time for thought and discussion, educated Greeks became some of the leading thinkers of the day. Philosophy, science,

Famed thinkers Plato and Aristotle are the central figures in Raphael's *The School of Athens*.

mathematics, literature, and drama all flourished.

A system of education also developed. During Greece's early history, children learned what they needed to know from their parents. Some boys from wealthy families may have had tutors hired from among the lower classes as well. Schools were established around the time democracy appeared. In Athens, boys began school at the age of seven. They learned reading, writing, physical education, and music. The various subjects were often taught at separate schools, and not all students had to study all subjects. At the age of 13, many boys from wealthy families went on to study with a teacher called a sophist. Sophists traveled from city to city to teach *rhetoric*, philosophy, and science. Some young men also studied at philosophical schools run by famed philosophers such as Socrates (c. 470–399 B.C.), Plato (428–348 B.C.), and Aristotle (384–322 B.C.).

Wealthy girls in most city-states received little (if any) formal education. They remained at home and learned to weave and carry out other household duties. Even once they were grown, upper-class women were expected to remain in

their homes much of the time. They might venture out to visit friends or relatives or to attend religious activities, but otherwise they took no part in public life. Although in some city-states, such as Athens, women were considered citizens, even there they did not have the right to vote, hold political office, or own land.

Women were considered inferior to men in Greek society. An unmarried girl remained under the control of her father. When she was about 15 years old, her father would arrange her marriage, often to a man she had never met. He might be twice her age. Once a woman was married, she came under the control of her husband. Her job was to provide him with sons and to supervise the slaves who took care of the household's cooking, cleaning, and childcare. Women also helped to make the family's clothing. It was not until the Hellenistic period (323–30 B.C.) that women were afforded more rights. Many upper-class women began to receive an education, and some even became philosophers or held minor political offices.

In contrast to the rest of the Greek world, girls in Sparta tended to experience more freedom.

A Greek wedding's ritual procession to the couple's home included music and dancing.

Most Spartan girls received an education similar to that of Spartan boys, which focused on physical training. In order to strengthen themselves for childbearing, Spartan girls participated in running, discus throwing, and wrestling. In Sparta, most girls did not get married until after the age of 18. In addition, Spartan women were allowed to leave the house. They did not have to make clothing and were allowed to own property.

Besides the husband and wife, a Greek household also generally consisted of two or three children, grandparents, unmarried female relatives, and slaves. Even among the aristocracy, all these people lived in a rather modest space. Greek homes were generally simple one- or two-story structures made of mud bricks. Most houses had a central courtyard surrounded by rooms on all four sides. The rooms were sparsely furnished. By the Hellenistic period, however, the houses of the wealthy were becoming more luxurious. They might be decorated with pieces of art such as marble sculptures, **mosaics**, or wall paintings.

The homes of most aristocrats also featured a special room known as the *andron*, or men's room. Although Greek families generally ate their meals together, the master of the home used this room to entertain only male guests at a sort of drinking party known as a symposium. The host of a symposium might begin by serving a grand meal of roast pig, oysters, scallops, eggs, and cakes. Guests ate their meal reclining on couches, with the food on a small table in front of them. After the food was cleared away, the guests drank wine, watched musicians, recited poetry, or discussed the ideas of the day.

Symposia were not held in Sparta, where men ate their meals together in dining clubs. All citizens were required to be members of a dining club—and to pay for that membership. Those who could no longer afford to maintain a membership in a dining club lost their citizenship and their position in society.

A WARRIOR'S LIFE

Greek city-states spent much of their time and energy on war, fighting with one another or with outside forces. For this reason, most developed strong, well-trained armies. Athens and other city-states also established powerful navies. Armies and navies defended city-states from outside invaders. They also helped conquer new lands, which could be plundered for *booty* or made to pay *tribute*. Sparta, for example, conquered the neighboring land of Messenia and forced its people to become helots, or slaves who provided the Spartans with food.

Until the 300s B.C., most city-states relied on amateur, or non-professional, citizen-soldiers for their armies. Citizen-soldiers lived at home and carried out

Ancient Greeks developed *triremes*, or warships with three banks of oars on each side of the boat.

their normal daily activities. They reported for military service only during times of war. In many city-states, all male citizens under the age of 60 were required to serve when called upon, even if it meant leaving their livelihood for weeks or months at a time. In most city-states, the army was made up of about 10,000 men at most, who were led by elected generals.

Although citizens were required to fight in the army, the government did not provide weapons or equipment. Because of this, armies were usually divided by class. The wealthiest, who could afford a horse, served in the cavalry (if the city-state had one). Other wealthy citizens served as hoplites. They went to battle in full armor, carrying a spear, a sword, and a shield made of wood and bronze. Because of the expense involved in purchasing such equipment, most hoplites were necessarily aristocrats. The poorest citizens made up the army division known as peltasts. These soldiers wore little to no armor and fought with javelins and slingshots. They carried shields made of woven twigs.

Training for military service usually began

around the age of 18. In Athens, the training period lasted two years. During this time, the young trainees were known as *ephebes*. Ephebes spent the first year of their training living in army barracks. They participated in athletic pursuits such as wrestling and track and practiced their weapons and battle skills. The second year, the ephebes served in a military post on the border of the Athenian region. Afterward, they were sent home until needed for war.

As in so many things, Sparta's army differed from that of other Greek city-states. Spartan citizens did not field an amateur army. Instead, nearly every citizen in Sparta was a professional hoplite. Spartans had no other occupation than to serve as foot soldiers. Since the helots provided Sparta's food, citizens were free to dedicate all their efforts toward military training and battle.

Preparation for life as a soldier began when a Spartan boy was seven years old, and he left his family to attend a military school. Life at the school was harsh, with nothing more than reeds for a bed and only a thin tunic for clothing year round. There was little food, and boys who wanted more were expected to steal it. The boys spent all

In the close combat typical of Greek warfare, hoplites employed their spears and shields.

day engaged in military exercises and physical exertion. Sometimes they were beaten, just to teach them to withstand pain. Spartan boys remained in military school until they were about 17 years old. They were required to spend the next two or three years on a special police force known as the *krypteia*. They lived in the wild, between Sparta and the lands of the helots. The krypteia randomly killed helots in order to keep the helot population panicked and submissive. Around the age of 20, a Spartan's military training came to an end. Even so, he continued to live in an army barracks until he was about 30. He also continued to participate in military training.

The dawn of the Hellenistic period saw the development of professional armies throughout much of the rest of Greece as well. Many city-states began to hire mercenaries, or soldiers who would fight for anyone who offered pay. In addition, some Greek soldiers (likely from lower classes) began to serve as mercenaries for Asian armies. Fighting offered them a full-time job.

In early Greek history, military battles were generally fought hand-to-hand. Around 700 B.C., though, Greek armies began to make use of the phalanx battle formation. In a phalanx, eight rows of armored hoplites stood close to one another. They held their shields up to form a "wall" against the enemy. As two phalanxes marched toward one another, the soldiers at the front raised their spears. Those in the back pushed forward, trying to break through the enemy's phalanx and cause the opposing soldiers to retreat. Phalanx battles were loud, dusty, and sweaty affairs. But they usually lasted less than an hour and resulted in relatively few casualties.

Although the life of a soldier could be hard, it had its rewards. Soldiers sometimes received booty from battle, a wage, or land, especially after the development of professional armies. Many soldiers fought for honor or to win glory or fame. Along with such glory often came political power.

Greeks rarely used the chariot for warfare but developed the popular sport of racing.

SERVING THE GODS

The Greeks incorporated religion into almost every part of their daily lives. They believed that their gods were everywhere and that they controlled everything. Greek religion did not set out a system of **morals**. Instead, it consisted of a series of prayers, sacrifices, and rituals that needed to be observed to get the gods' attention and keep them happy. If the gods were happy, they would help humans. If, on the other hand, people neglected to make sacrifices and prayers, the gods might ignore the people's needs or even bring disaster.

The Greeks believed in a number of different gods. The 12 main gods were known as the Olympians, because they were believed to live on Mount Olympus.

Built around 432 B.C., the Statue of Zeus at Olympia was more than 40 feet (12 m) high.

Zeus was the king of the Olympic gods. Each city-state had its own *patron* god or goddess. The patron goddess of Athens, for example, was Athena. The Greeks also worshiped a number of minor gods, as well as heroes. Often, humans who had done great things, such as founding a city, were made heroes after their deaths.

All Greek citizens honored the gods as part of their daily life. They kept statues of the gods in their home to watch over their family. They also said prayers and left offerings for the gods at one or more *altars* in their house. The master of the household led a family in its religious observations.

While the household altar was important for family rituals, temples served as places of public ritual and worship. Each city-state had a temple dedicated to its patron deity. The Parthenon in Athens, for example, was dedicated to Athena. Other temples throughout the city honored different gods. Since a temple was believed to be the home of a god, people did not step inside it, except during festivals. Instead, they worshiped the god at an altar located outside the temple.

A large group of priests and priestesses oversaw

public worship. Each priest or priestess served a specific god or goddess at a specific temple. There were few universal qualifications for becoming a priest or priestess. For some priesthoods, a person had to come from an aristocratic family, and the priesthood was passed down from father to son or mother to daughter. For other priesthoods, age mattered. Some gods were served by young boys, others by old women. In general, gods were served by male priests and goddesses by female priestesses.

There were a number of ways to become a priest or priestess. A lottery was held to determine some priesthoods, while others were elected. A few wealthy Greeks even bought their way into a priesthood. Some priests served for life, while others had terms as short as a year.

Although priests were not necessary for worship—anyone could carry out a sacrifice or pray—they helped to ensure that such rituals were carried out properly. Animal sacrifices were meant to honor the gods, thank the gods, or make a request of the gods. In most cases, sheep or goats were sacrificed, although bulls, dogs, birds, or fish were sometimes used as well. At the end of the

At the Temple of Athena, worshipers entreated the goddess for wisdom and victory.

Did You Know?

WEALTHY GREEKS

WERE CALLED UPON

TO PAY SPECIAL

TAXES THAT FUNDED

THEATER FESTIVALS

OR THE OPERATION

OF WARSHIPS.

sacrifice, the meat from the animal was shared by everyone in attendance.

Sacrifices were often carried out at religious festivals dedicated to a particular god. In Athens alone, citizens spent at least 60 days each year participating in festivals. People from all walks of life attended the festivals. No expense was spared: festivals were the biggest expenditure for a city-state each year, other than war. In addition to sacrifices, festivals included processions, feasts, and music. Sometimes there were athletic or theater contests as well.

The largest festivals were Panhellenic. In other words, they included people from all over the Greek world. These festivals often included athletic games, in which athletes honored the gods by showing off their physical skills. The Olympic Games, for example, were held every four years at Olympia in honor of Zeus. All athletes at the Olympics were male—married women were not even allowed to watch the Olympics. Unmarried women participated in foot races at their own

games. Most Olympic athletes were aristocrats who had the spare time to train for events such as races or wrestling matches. Olympic winners were rewarded with a crown of wild olives. They were also honored throughout the Greek world and might receive large payments from their home city-state.

While some priests attended to festivals, sacrifices, and games, a few served as oracles. These special priests were seen as spokespeople for a specific god. If a person needed advice, he or she asked an oracle. The oracle then gave the person the god's answer. The Greeks placed much importance on oracles. They consulted oracles before undertaking major events such as a war or for minor daily decisions such as planting crops.

For their services, priests received a salary, part of the sacrificial meat, and housing. But the greatest reward was social prestige. For women, especially, serving as a priestess was one of the few ways to make a mark on Greek society.

Festivals included contests and plays in theaters (opposite) as well as religious rituals (above).

WORKING FOR A LIVING

In aristocratic circles, the idea of working for a living was looked down upon. But most Greeks could not afford a life of leisure. Among those who had to work for a living, the ideal was to work for themselves. Working for another person—even for pay—was seen as being too close to slavery.

In most-city states, the majority of the population worked as farmers. Most had small farms of two to five acres (0.8–2 ha). Their goal was to raise enough food to feed their family. If they had extra, they might sell it in the market, but this was not their primary concern. Farmers generally did not live on their farms. Instead, a farmer lived in a village and rode his donkey out to his fields each day. Farming

Ancient Greek farmers harvested wheat, barley, olives, and grapes from the rocky soil.

could be a difficult life in Greece, with its poor soil and dry climate. Sometimes small farmers could not afford to keep their land. They often sold out to wealthy landowners. They might continue to work the land as tenant farmers, paying a portion of the crop to the wealthy landowner each year.

Although farming was the main source of income for most citizens, most larger cities (aside from Sparta) also had thriving industries and markets in which many people worked. Some of those people were slaves or foreigners known as *metics*, but free citizens also participated in industry. City dwellers might work as shipbuilders, blacksmiths, jewelers, bankers, construction workers, or artisans.

Artisans, or craftsmen, made pottery, textiles, shoes, lamps, and more. Usually, boys learned a craft from their fathers. Some artisans also took on **apprentices**. An artisan generally had a small workshop, where he might work alone or with a handful of slaves. The workshop might be attached to his house. The front of the shop might also contain a store for selling the goods produced there. In many city-states, the people who

worked in similar crafts lived near one another. Some artisans might leave the business operations to a slave rather than work in the workshop himself.

Although Greek artists and sculptors produced great works that would influence art long into the future, at the time they were regarded as mere artisans because they worked with their hands. They generally did not have their own workshops but instead traveled to wherever work was available. Many produced pieces for the state or for wealthy patrons. In order to avoid being regarded as an employee, they were careful not to accept too many projects from a single patron. Although a few artists achieved fame, many others did not even sign their works.

Although artisans were looked down upon by the wealthy, they likely felt pride in their own work. Some tombstones even contain inscriptions praising a person's skill at a particular craft. While many artisans probably struggled financially, some could become wealthy and earn a certain level of respect.

That respect was generally not shared by doctors, who had low status because they worked

Artisans depicted scenes of Greek life on objects such as kraters, a type of vase.

HOMER'S **EPIC POEMS**

THE *ILIAD* AND THE

ODYSSEY RECORD ORAL

TRADITIONS ABOUT

DAILY LIFE IN GREECE

BEFORE THE DARK AGE.

for wages. Despite this fact, Greek doctors made many advancements. They set up medical schools and introduced the idea that illnesses were caused by physical forces rather than by the gods. Like doctors, teachers were looked down upon as laborers. Most received little pay—or respect—for their services, although sophists could charge high prices for their instruction.

Although their work kept laborers busy, most still found time to enjoy other pursuits. Those who worked for themselves could close their shops and have time off whenever they chose. Commoners participated in festivals, attended the theater, and spent time in political discussions. During the period of democracy, they also attended the assembly and served in political offices, if their name was drawn by lot.

By the 400s B.C., the children of many commoners began to attend school, at least until they were needed at home or in their fathers' businesses. As with the elite, education was probably limited to boys for much of Greek history. Even so, common women did not face nearly as many restrictions as upper-class women. Working-class women were not confined to the house. They went to the market and fetched water from the public fountain. Some worked in their husband's workshop or took jobs outside the home as nannies, nurses, perfumers, or cloth-makers. On top of this, they took care of the household.

At home, working-class people enjoyed different levels of comfort. Some lived in houses similar in style to those of the wealthy but smaller and made of lower-quality materials. These homes did not have a men's room for holding symposia. Instead, that space might be used as a shop. Poorer commoners lived in one-room homes or in poorly built apartment buildings. The food of the working class was generally plain: bread, porridge (boiled grain), soup, olive oil, and fruits and vegetables.

Occasionally, a commoner became wealthy enough to marry into an aristocratic family. But for the most part, aristocrats jealously protected their position in society, rarely allowing newcomers to join their ranks.

The hero of the *Odyssey* is Odysseus, the legendary king of the Greek island of Ithaca.

THE BOTTOM RUNGS

At the bottom of the social ladder in ancient Greece were noncitizens. These included foreign residents known as metics, slaves, and, in Sparta, helots. Metics were people who were not born in the city-state in which they lived. Although they were allowed to live there, they were not given the rights of citizenship. In Athens, they could not own property or participate in politics. In addition, metics had to pay a special tax and serve in the military.

The majority of metics settled in or near Athens. They were usually attracted to the city's thriving economy. Many metics engaged in crafts and manufacturing. In addition, trade in many city-states was controlled almost entirely by the metics. Metics purchased goods

Slaves took part in harvesting olives and pressing them for oil to be sold or traded.

from foreign traders or from local craftsmen and farmers, and then they sold these goods in the agora. Although traders were looked down upon for making a profit off others, they were a necessary part of life in most city-states. They sold grain imported from Egypt, Sicily, and southern Russia, and traded for olive oil, perfume, grapes, apples, flowers, fish, iron, exotic animals, and even slaves.

Metics freely joined citizens in the social activities of the city-state. They took part in religious festivals and attended the theater. Occasionally, metics became rich through trade. In some cases, the city-state might allow wealthy metics to purchase citizenship.

Although metics were not afforded the same rights as citizens, they were still free. Slaves, on the other hand, were not. As far as scholars can tell, slavery existed in ancient Greece from the civilization's earliest days. At first, there may have been few slaves. In the sixth century B.C., however, the number of slaves began to grow rapidly. By the 300s B.C., there may have been up to 100,000 slaves in Athens, probably representing about a third of the city-state's population.

Owning slaves was a sign of status in the Greek world. All but the poorest Athenians strove to own at least one slave. The wealthy might have 10 or 20 slaves, and the very richest members of society could have up to 1,000.

There were several ways in which a person could be made a slave. A child born to a slave woman was automatically a slave. In addition, poor families might sell their children into slavery. Sometimes families left unwanted babies (especially girls) out in the open to die. Slave traders might take in these infants and raise them for sale. Peoples conquered in war were often made slaves as well. Kidnappers and pirates also snatched people to be sold in the slave market.

Slaves carried out a variety of jobs. Some worked in households as nannies, tutors, weavers, cooks, cleaners, or gardeners. Slaves also served as skilled and unskilled workers in workshops. In some cases, owners made slaves the managers of their craft, trade, or banking enterprises. Some of these slaves had their own homes and earned money; they were obligated to give part of their income to their masters. Other slaves worked the

Workers carried out the plans of architects for the Acropolis temples in the 400s B.C.

fields of wealthy landowners. A number of slaves also belonged to the state. They kept records, managed public buildings, constructed roads, or served on the police force.

The conditions under which slaves worked varied greatly. Some masters treated their slaves well. Household slaves often grew close to the families they served. But since slaves were thought of as property, an owner could starve or beat his slaves if he wished. The worst conditions were faced by the slaves in silver mines. They were made to work long shifts, with little food. Most had a short lifespan.

Once enslaved, most people remained in slavery for life. But a few managed to save enough money to buy their freedom. Some were also freed when their master died. Freed slaves became metics.

Even more than other city-states, Sparta relied on its slave population to maintain its way of life. Around 715 B.C., Sparta conquered the nearby land of Messenia. The Spartans claimed the Messenians—along with earlier-conquered peoples from Laconia—as helots. The helots were owned by the Spartan government, and the government distributed them among the people. Even after being made slaves, the helots continued to live in their homelands and work the fields. But they were expected to give half of their harvest to their Spartan masters. Helots also carried out Sparta's limited trade and occasionally were called upon to serve in Sparta's military.

Although they were allowed to remain in their communities, helots had few rights. Each year, Sparta officially declared war on them. This meant that a Spartan could kill a helot and not face punishment. Because the helot population was so large—possibly up to seven times the size of the Spartan population—Spartans feared a helot revolt. The Spartan military was dedicated to preventing this. Even so, the helots managed to stage a number of uprisings. In 369 B.C., the Messenian helots were freed; the Laconians were freed in the 100s B.C.

LASTING INFLUENCE

By the Hellenistic period, the Greek world had expanded to include places as far away as Egypt, ***Persia***, and Macedonia. Kings of Greek and Macedonian ancestry ruled the Hellenistic kingdoms, and Greek aristocrats served in their governments. Lavish spending by the ruling monarchies weakened these kingdoms. Around 146 B.C., Rome took over Macedonia and began to conquer Greek lands. Within little more than 100 years, Rome wielded control over the entire Greek world.

Instead of destroying Greek culture, the Romans embraced it. They imitated Greek architecture, painting, and sculpture, read Greek books and plays, and followed Greek scientific practices. For most Greeks,

The U.S. Capitol's Corinthian columns were inspired by classical Greek architecture.

life continued as it had in the past. Aristocratic Greeks no longer held political power, but their wealth and position in society were secure. Some even became Roman citizens. But some Greeks captured in war were made Roman slaves. Well-educated Greek slaves served as doctors, teachers, musicians, and artists in Rome. Their education likely enabled them to receive better treatment over other slaves.

Eventually, the Roman Empire split into eastern and western halves. When the Western Roman Empire fell in A.D. 476, Greece remained part of the eastern, or Byzantine, empire. But Greece had been weakened by attacks from **barbarian** invaders, and its culture began to decline. In addition, the Byzantine Empire was a **Christian** empire, and in A.D. 529, the emperor Justinian closed the non-Christian philosophical schools in Athens. Some scholars consider this the end of the ancient Greek culture.

The culture's influence lived on, however. From the 1300s to the 1600s, much of Europe

experienced a period of cultural reawakening known as the Renaissance. Painters, sculptors, and thinkers revived ancient Greek styles and ideas, creating some of the great masterpieces of the modern Western world.

Greek influence didn't end with the Renaissance, either. Today, many buildings—including the United States Capitol—are based on Greek architecture. Drama and other forms of Western literature have their roots in ancient Greece, as do philosophy and science. And in establishing some of the world's first democracies, the Greeks laid the foundations for modern systems of government.

Today, ruins from the Greek civilization still stand in many places where the ancient Greeks once lived. Those ruins—along with writings from the time—attest to a society in which everyone had his or her own place in the social order. Despite the divisions between social classes, everyone contributed to the rich culture known as ancient Greece.

c. 1400 b.c.	—	The Mycenaean culture begins to flourish on the Greek mainland.
c. 1200 b.c.	—	The Mycenaeans fall, and Greek-speaking people move into the mainland.
c. 800 b.c.	—	Greek city-states begin to be established.
776 b.c.	—	The first Olympic Games are held.
c. 750 b.c.	—	The poet Homer is believed to have written the epic poems the *Iliad* and the *Odyssey*.
715 b.c.	—	Sparta conquers Messenia, making its people—along with the earlier-conquered Laconians—serve as helots.
650 b.c.	—	A period of rule by tyrants begins in many city-states.
594 b.c.	—	The Athenian magistrate Solon introduces reforms that give more power to persons who are not part of the aristocracy, thus paving the way for democracy.
546 b.c.	—	The first tyrant in Athens takes power.
508/507 b.c.	—	Athens becomes a democracy.
487 b.c.	—	In Athens, magistrates begin to be chosen by lottery.
482 b.c.	—	Athens builds a naval fleet.
478 b.c.	—	The classical period of Greek history begins, marking a high point in ancient Greek culture.
464 b.c.	—	Helots revolt after an earthquake in Sparta.
460 b.c.	—	An Athenian named Pericles begins to dominate Athenian politics, introducing ambitious building projects.
404 b.c.	—	Sparta becomes the most powerful city-state in Greece after defeating Athens in the Peloponnesian War.
388 b.c.	—	The Athenian philosopher Plato establishes a philosophical school known as the Academy.
338 b.c.	—	Macedonia takes over Athens, leading to the Hellenistic period.
146 b.c.	—	Rome begins to take over Greece.
a.d. 529	—	Emperor Justinian closes philosophical schools in Athens, and the ancient Greek culture comes to an end.

ALTARS: special tables used for carrying out religious rituals

APPRENTICES: people who learn a job or craft by working under the guidance of someone with more experience

ARISTOCRATS: people at the top of a society, usually by virtue of being born into an elite family

BARBARIAN: relating to people who lived outside the Roman Empire and who were considered inferior by the Romans

BOOTY: money or goods taken from a defeated enemy in war

CHRISTIAN: related to Christianity, a religion based on the teachings and person of Jesus of Nazareth; it professes that Jesus is the son of God, that he died for the sins of all people, and that he rose from the dead

EPIC POEMS: long poems that tell the story of a hero

EXILED: forced to leave one's homeland

MORALS: rules relating to right and wrong behaviors

MOSAICS: pictures made from tiny pieces of glass or stone

OLIGARCHY: a form of government led by a small, elite group

PATRON: a special protector or supporter

PERSIA: an empire that covered much of southwestern Asia, including present-day Iran, until it was conquered by Macedonia in 330 B.C.

PHILOSOPHICAL: relating to philosophy, or the study of ethics, logic, and other ideas

RHETORIC: the art and study of speaking and writing well to persuade others

TENANT: someone who rents a home or land from the property owner

TREATIES: agreements between two countries, often regarding war, alliances, or trade

TRIBUTE: a payment made by a weaker nation to a stronger one, often because of conquest or for protection

TRUCE: an agreement to stop fighting for a time

TUNIC: a knee-length, loose-fitting shirt

TYRANNY: a form of government led by a single ruler who holds complete power, with no restrictions

Selected Bibliography

Budin, Stephanie Lynn. *The Ancient Greeks: New Perspectives*. Santa Barbara, Calif.: ABC-CLIO, 2004.

Connolly, Peter, and Hazel Dodge. *The Ancient City: Life in Classical Athens & Rome*. New York: Oxford University Press, 1998.

Evans, James Allan. *Daily Life in the Hellenistic Age: From Alexander to Cleopatra*. Westport, Conn.: Greenwood Press, 2008.

Garland, Robert. *Daily Life of the Ancient Greeks*. Westport, Conn.: Greenwood Press, 2009.

Jenkins, Ian. *Greek and Roman Life*. Cambridge, Mass.: Harvard University Press, 1986.

Moulton, Carroll, ed. *Ancient Greece and Rome: An Encyclopedia for Students*. Vols. 1–4. New York: Scribner's, 1998.

Nardo, Don, ed. *Living in Ancient Greece*. San Diego: Greenhaven Press, 2004.

Pomeroy, Sarah B., Stanley M. Burstein, Walter Donlan, and Jennifer Tolbert Roberts. *Ancient Greece: A Political, Social, and Cultural History*. New York: Oxford University Press, 1999.

Websites

THE ANCIENT OLYMPICS

http://www.perseus.tufts.edu/Olympics/

Find out what events the ancient Greek Olympics involved, and learn more about some of the athletes who competed in them.

THE BRITISH MUSEUM: ANCIENT GREECE

http://www.ancientgreece.co.uk/menu.html

Learn more about daily life in ancient Greece, try out interactive tours, and take a turn steering a warship.

Note: Every effort has been made to ensure that the websites listed above are suitable for children, that they have educational value, and that they contain no inappropriate material. However, because of the nature of the Internet, it is impossible to guarantee that these sites will remain active indefinitely or that their contents will not be altered.